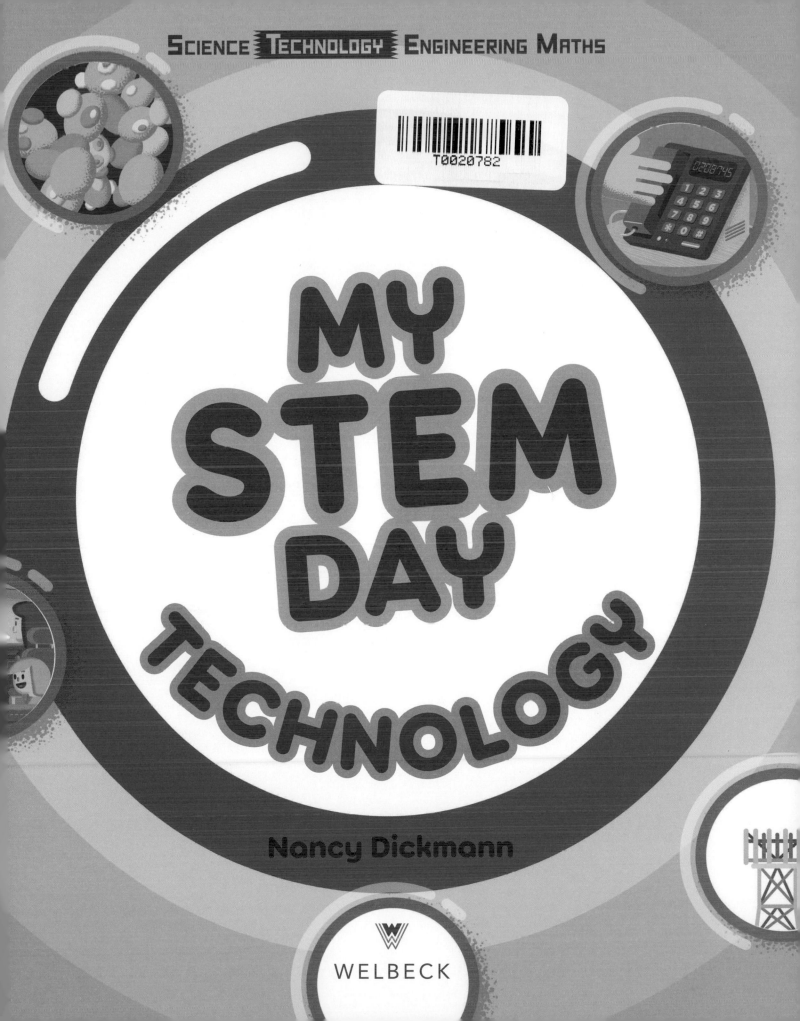

SCIENCE TECHNOLOGY ENGINEERING MATHS

T0020782

MY STEM DAY

TECHNOLOGY

Nancy Dickmann

WELBECK

Published in 2021 by Welbeck Children's Books

An Imprint of Welbeck Children's Limited,
part of Welbeck Publishing Group.
20 Mortimer Street London W1T 3JW

ISBN: 978 1 78312 655 2
Printed in Dongguan, China

Design Manager: **Emily Clarke**
Editorial Manager: **Joff Brown**
Executive Editors: **Selina Wood and Nancy Dickmann**
Design: **Jake da'Costa and WildPixel Ltd.**
Picture research: **Steve Behan**
Production: **Nicola Davey**
Editorial Consultant: **Jack Challoner**

AUTHOR
Nancy Dickmann has written more than 150 non-fiction books for children, specializing in science and history. Before becoming an author, she worked for many years as an editor and publisher of children's books.

STEM CONSULTANT
Jack Challoner has a degree in physics and trained as a science and maths teacher before moving to the Education Unit at London's Science Museum. He now writes science and technology books and performs science shows in museums and schools.

ILLUSTRATOR
Alejandro@KJA-artists is a South American artist. He worked for many years as an Art Director in the advertising industry, but one day he decided to become an illustrator following his true passion. Now he dedicates every single day to create happy images that try to put a smile on your face.

The publishers would like to thank the following sources for their kind permission to reproduce the pictures in the book.

Page 17: bergamont/Shutterstock; 20: Bart_J/Shutterstock; 32: Vangelis_Vassalakis/Shutterstock; 33 (top): Oleksandr Kostiuchenko/Shutterstock, (bottom): Sergio Delle Vedove/Shutterstock; 54: finchfocus/Shutterstock; 56: mohamadhafizmohamad/Shutterstock

Adult supervision is recommended for all activities.

MY STEM DAY

TECHNOLOGY

Nancy Dickmann

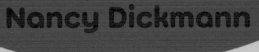
WELBECK

CONTENTS

TICK, TOCK!

What is STEM? 6

Rise and shine! 8

Make a pendulum 10

Toasty tech 12

Build a circuit 14

Biotech breakfast 16

Yeast in action....................18

UNLOCK THE SECRETS OF YEAST!

Over the airwaves 20

Make a sound booster 22

Out and about 24

Find your location 26

Tap and swipe 28

Make your own stylus 30

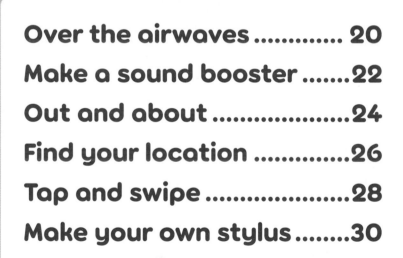

The write stuff 32

Investigating ink colors 34

Super scanners 36

Make your own barcode 38

A cellular world 40

Blocking signals 42

Snack time! 44

Microwave heat test 46

LEARN TO DECODE A BARCODE!

BEEP! BEEP!

Helping out 48

Be a vacuum cleaner! 50

Simple machines 52

Lifting with pulleys 54

Bedtime brush! 56

Is electric better? 58

Technology everywhere! .. 60

Quiz time! 61

Puzzle activity answers 62

RING! RING!

10:15

WHAT IS STEM?

BOOM! BOOM!

STEM is everywhere in our lives. But it's not all about flowers! Instead, STEM is short for **Science**, **Technology**, **Engineering** and **Mathematics**.

Have you ever ridden a bicycle, heated a snack in the microwave or listened to the radio? If so, you've already come across **STEM**. Scientists and engineers over the years have used their knowledge and skills to develop tools, structures and processes that we use every day.

Are you curious about the world around you? Do you love to ask questions and try out new ideas? Maybe you're a whiz at spotting patterns, solving problems and finding out how things work. If you try something that doesn't work out the first time, do you try again with a different approach? If so, you'll love the world of **STEM**.

Technology is one of the four branches of STEM. It is all about making useful devices and finding new ways of doing things. Technology can be simple, like a wheel or a pencil. It can also be complex, like a supercomputer or an airplane.

We depend on technology in our daily lives. We have gadgets to make jobs easier, entertain us and keep us connected with each other. Once you know where to look, you'll spot examples of technology everywhere you go!

What about the rest of **STEM**? Well, **Science** investigates the natural world and all its mysteries. **Engineering** is all about solving problems to create structures and machines. **Mathematics** is the study of numbers and shapes. These subjects work together to explore and create incredible things!

THE STEM DAY TEAM

SCIENCE   TECHNOLOGY   ENGINEERING   MATH

Rise and Shine!

Beeeep! A new day is starting and an alarm rings so you won't be late for school. We take clocks for granted, but they are very useful pieces of technology!

DING! DING!

YAWN!

BEEP! BEEP!

10:15

analog clock

digital clock

There are two main types of clock: analog and digital. An analog clock shows the time by the position of its "hands", which point to numbers or lines on a round "face". Digital clocks show the time just as numbers, such as 10:15.

Clocks and watches can be very different from each other inside. Some have gears (interlocking wheels) and springs inside to make the hands move. These clocks might run on a battery, or they might need to be wound up from time to time.

gears

TICK TOCK! TICK TOCK!

Some clocks have swinging pendulums to keep the gears moving at the right speed.

battery

quartz crystal

gears

Many modern clocks use a crystal called quartz to keep time. The battery sends a current of electricity through the crystal. The electricity makes the crystal vibrate, or move quickly back and forth. Quartz always vibrates at the same rate, so once you know how many vibrations there are in a second, electronic circuits can use them to count seconds.

Before clocks were invented, people had other ways of telling the time. Sundials created shadows as the Sun moved across the sky, showing the time. Water clocks used flowing water and hourglasses used flowing sand. There were even candle clocks, where the height of a burning candle showed how many hours had passed!

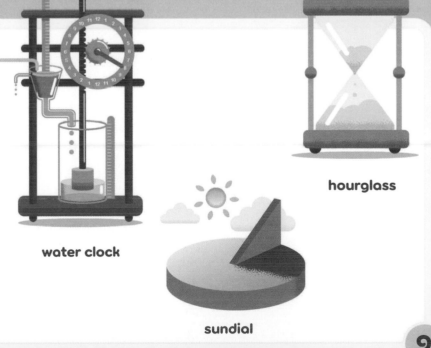

water clock

sundial

hourglass

Make a pendulum

You will need:

- string
- scissors
- a pencil and paper
- a table
- heavy books
- metal nuts or washers
- a stopwatch
- a ruler
- a friend to help

A **pendulum** is a hanging weight that can swing freely back and forth. It works in a way that is perfect for clocks, as this experiment will show you!

What to do:

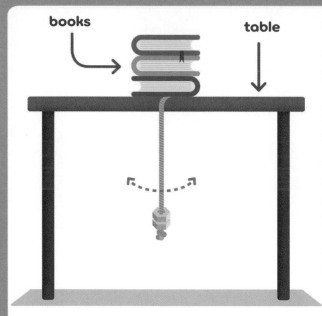

books

table

1. Cut a piece of string about 2 feet long..

2. Tie a few nuts or washers to one end.

3. Put the other end of the string on the table and use a pile of books to hold it in place. Your pendulum should swing freely.

4. Pull the pendulum back about 2 feet and release it. Ask your friend to time one minute with the stopwatch while you count how many times the pendulum swings back and forth. Make a note of the number.

5. Pull the pendulum back again, but only about 1 foot this time. Count the number of swings in one minute. Is it the same or different?

6. Adjust the length of the string until you have a pendulum that swings 60 times in a minute.

The time it takes for a pendulum to swing back and forth is always the same, no matter how far you pull it back. Only changing the length of a pendulum will change the speed of the swing.

Puzzle activity

Analog and digital clocks show time in different ways. Work out the time on each of these analog clocks, then fill in the bars to show the same time on the digital clock.

EXAMPLE

Toasty tech

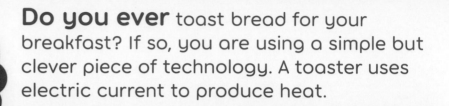

Do you ever toast bread for your breakfast? If so, you are using a simple but clever piece of technology. A toaster uses electric current to produce heat.

Electric current is the movement of electric charge. Inside wires, tiny particles called electrons carry electric charge. In some materials, electrons can flow freely, so they can carry electric current very well. In other materials, the electrons are not so free to move, and little or no current can flow.

RUMBLE! RUMBLE!

Electrons can only move if the wires form a closed loop, called a circuit. Inside the slots of a toaster you'll see rows of wires on each side. They are all connected to form an electric circuit inside the toaster.

handle

wires

current flows in a circuit

WATCH OUT!

Never stick anything—particularly your fingers — inside a toaster. Electric current could flow through you, giving you a very nasty shock!

ORANGE MEANS HOT!

The wires inside a toaster are thin, so the electrons do not have much space, and they bump into each other, and into the atoms of which the metal is made. This generates lots of heat. The wires start to glow red-orange, and they give off heat that toasts your bread.

Always ask an adult to pour the kettle!

An electric kettle works in a similar way. Resistance is provided by a coil of metal at the bottom of the kettle. Once the water boils, the coil moves and the kettle switches off automatically. Time for a cup of hot cocoa!

Build a circuit

Sharp scissors! WATCH OUT!

In a toaster, kettle, or any other electric gadget, electric current flows through a closed circuit. You can build your own circuit to turn on a light bulb like this.

bulb

wire

electrons move from the negative to the positive end of the battery

battery

What to do:

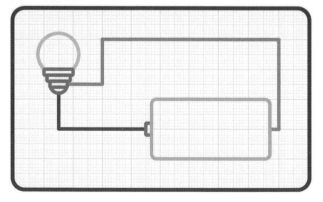

1. Draw your circuit on paper. It should be a loop, with one wire going from the battery to the light bulb, and one going from the light bulb to the battery.

2. Ask an adult to cut the copper wire into two roughly equal pieces and strip about half an inch of plastic coating from each of the four ends.

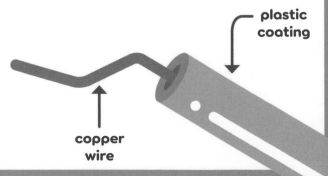

plastic coating

copper wire

3. Tape the end of one wire to the sticky-out lump (positive terminal) at the top of the battery. Tape the other end to the bottom of the metal part of the bulb.

4. Tape one end of the other wire to the opposite end (negative terminal) of the battery.

5. Holding the other end of this wire by the plastic coating, touch the metal end to the metal part of the light bulb.

HOLD BY PLASTIC COATING!

When you touch the wire to the light bulb, it completes the circuit—the electrons can travel through the tiny wire inside the bulb —and the bulb should light up. When you take it away, the circuit is broken and the bulb will go out.

Puzzle activity

What's for breakfast? Follow the twisting lines to find out which breakfast food is cooking inside each of these three toasters.

Biotech breakfast

Bread and yogurt seem like pretty simple foods. But they are both examples of biotechnology: using living ingredients and processes to make products.

muscle cells

Your body is made of trillions of building blocks called cells. But some living things have just one cell. These microorganisms are too small to see without a microscope. Even so, some of them can be very useful.

MICROSCOPE

How yeast cells look under a microscope

Did you know that one of the ingredients in bread is alive? To make dough rise, bakers use a single-celled fungus called yeast. When yeast is mixed with the warm water in dough, it becomes active, causing bubbles. Here's how...

yeast in dough

bubbles in dough

The yeast cells feed on the flour in the dough. As a waste product, they give off a gas called carbon dioxide. The carbon dioxide forms tiny bubbles that get trapped in the dough. As the yeast gives off more and more carbon dioxide, the dough rises up.

When you cut a slice of bread, you can sometimes see the pockets formed by the carbon dioxide bubbles.

pocket

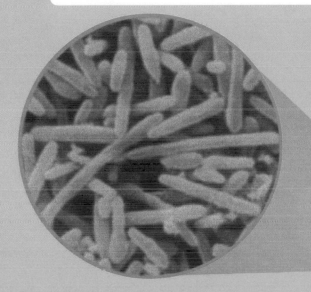

The bacteria in yogurt are much smaller than the point of a pin and can only be seen with a microscope.

Yogurt uses a different type of single-celled microorganism: bacteria. In factories, bacteria are added to milk. The bacteria feed on a sweet substance called lactose in the milk. This then turns into a sour substance called lactic acid. This acid changes the flavor and the texture of the milk. It turns it into yogurt!

Yeast in action

You will need:

- an adult helper
- 4 cups bread flour
- 1 teaspoon salt
- 2 teaspoons dried yeast
- 2 tablespoons soft butter
- 1/3 cup milk
- 1/3 cup milk water

Give making your own bread rolls a try, using yeast to make them puffy and yummy!

What to do:

1. Put the flour, salt, and yeast into a bowl, and mix together.

2. Add the butter and rub it in with your fingers until the mixture looks like breadcrumbs.

3. Add the water to the milk, warm the mixture a little in the microwave, then pour it into the bowl.

4. Mix everything together and mold the dough into a ball.

5. Dust your worktop with flour and knead the dough for 10 minutes.

6. Put the dough in a clean bowl, cover it with a dish towel, and leave it in a warm place for about an hour to rise.

7. When it's nice and puffy, punch the dough down and divide it into eight pieces. Roll each piece into a ball.

8. Put the balls on a baking tray and leave them for an hour to rise again.

9. Ask an adult to heat the oven to 425°F.

8–10 minutes

10. Bake the rolls for 8–10 minutes.

Now enjoy eating your bread rolls. Can you see how the yeast made the dough rise and made your rolls plump and puffy?

Puzzle activity

Can you find all these words related to bread and yogurt hidden in the word search grid?

BACTERIA
BIOTECHNOLOGY
BREAD
CARBON DIOXIDE
CELLS
DOUGH
FUNGUS
LACTIC ACID
LACTOSE
MICROORGANISM
MILK
WASTE PRODUCT
YEAST
YOGURT

C	G	I	F	M	Y	U	Z	O	P	F	J	Y	N
K	B	I	O	T	E	C	H	N	O	L	O	G	Y
S	R	H	F	C	A	A	K	Y	B	A	I	L	O
P	E	X	Q	L	S	R	J	B	E	C	V	R	G
D	A	S	N	T	T	B	F	Z	O	T	U	N	U
X	D	O	U	G	H	O	S	H	T	O	B	C	R
N	Q	C	G	M	P	N	W	I	K	S	Z	E	T
U	D	G	E	H	J	D	A	V	S	E	O	L	T
W	E	N	U	Y	T	I	G	J	L	I	B	L	X
A	M	I	C	R	O	O	R	G	A	N	I	S	M
F	R	A	V	H	T	X	N	U	X	W	O	B	I
U	O	L	A	C	T	I	C	A	C	I	D	T	L
N	H	B	T	C	E	D	H	G	L	U	A	B	K
G	F	W	A	S	T	E	P	R	O	D	U	C	T
U	Y	V	K	E	G	I	P	V	F	T	A	P	M
S	K	E	N	A	B	A	C	T	E	R	I	A	S

Over the airwaves

YEAH, YEAH, YEAH!

SMASH!

CRASH!

CRASH!

SMASH!

Do you listen to the radio in the car on the way to school? Radios pick up invisible signals called radio waves that travel through the air and turn them into sounds we can hear.

Sound is a type of energy, just like light or heat. Objects produce sound when they vibrate. When you hit a drum, it vibrates. The vibrations are passed into the air as sound waves. The waves continue to travel through the air until they reach your ears.

Radios don't produce their own music—they have to pick up a signal first. At a radio station, sound waves are turned into electrical signals and sent out, coded into radio waves, from a radio tower. Radios have an aerial that receives the radio waves. The radio then turns the signal back into sound.

radio mast

When a DJ broadcasts over the radio, the sound waves of their voice are turned into an electrical signal, which is coded into radio waves sent through the air.

ON AIR ▶

1. A DJ's voice travels as sound waves. Sound waves are turned into electrical signals coded into radio waves.

2. Radio waves are transmitted (sent out) from a radio mast.

3. The aerial on a radio captures the radio waves and they are decoded, producing a sound signal. The radio's speaker produces sound waves you can hear.

The signal that a radio receives is very weak. To make a bigger sound, a radio amplifies (boosts) the signal. It sends it through a speaker, which has a cone made of a flexible material. The cone vibrates, producing powerful sound waves that travel through the air and to your ears.

Make a sound booster

You will need:

- an adult helper
- a small radio
- large containers you can put your radio inside, such as a ceramic bowl, glass jar, plastic bottle cut in half, or sheet of paper
- scissors
- tape
- a pencil and paper

Radios and stereos amplify sound signals so that you can hear sound more easily. But you don't need an expensive speaker to make sounds louder—you can try boosting your radio's sound yourself with a few things from around the house!

What to do:

1. Turn on your radio. Notice how loud and clear the sound is.

2. Try putting your radio into a large glass jar, large ceramic bowl, or any other container you can put your radio inside completely.

3. Do any of the containers make the sound from your radio louder? Make a note of your results. Do any of the containers muffle the sound?

4. Try wrapping a long sheet of paper or poster board in a cone shape around the speaker of your radio. Make a note of the volume of the sound from your radio. What do you notice?

You will probably find that different materials and shapes produced different results. A ceramic bowl often boosts sound because its hard surface and round shape help to reflect the sound waves toward you, rather than absorb the waves or pass them outward.

Puzzle activity

The radios on the shelf in a shop may all look different, but they have many of the same parts. All radios have a power source, an aerial, and a dial for tuning. Inside, they have a speaker to amplify the sound. Can you spot five differences between these two radios?

Out and about

TA-DAH!

You know the way to school, but what about finding new places? Your parents might use satnav (satellite navigation) in the car. This amazing technology uses satellites in space to show you the way.

A smartphone or satnav device is programmed with road maps. It also has complicated programs that help it work out the best route from one place to another. But in order to plan your route, your device has to know where you are! It can work out your position by receiving signals from satellites orbiting high above the ground, in space.

There are about 30 navigation satellites in orbit, traveling around Earth. Each one follows a different path as it loops around the planet. No matter where you are, you will always be in range of at least three satellites.

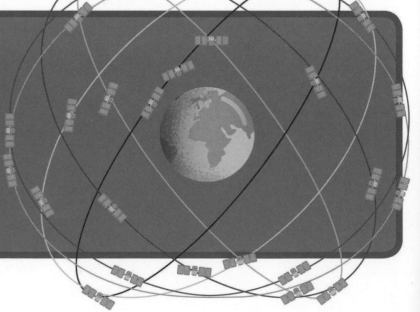

1. Each satellite sends out a signal in the form of radio waves that travel incredibly fast. Your smartphone or satnav device calculates how long it takes for a signal to reach it. That helps it work out how far away the satellite is.

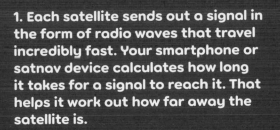

2. Using one satellite is not enough to work out your position. You could trace a large circle on Earth's surface that is exactly the same distance from the satellite. But if you find the distance from a second satellite and draw another circle, they will only intersect at two points.

3. Adding a third satellite will pinpoint your location. There will only be one place on Earth where the distance circles from all three satellites meet. That's where you are!

You will need:

- an adult helper
- graph or squared paper
- a pencil
- a compass

Sharp compasses! WATCH OUT!

The way that satellite navigation pinpoints a location is called trilateration. You don't need a network of satellites to have a go at it! You can try your own simple version using a pencil and paper.

What to do:

1. Mark a dot on your graph paper where four squares meet. This represents one of your satellites.

2. Count 12 squares to the right and 3 squares up, then make another dot

3. Count 9 squares to the right of the first dot and 13 squares down. Make another dot. You now have three satellites.

4. With an adult's help, put the point of your compass on the first dot and open it up until the pencil is touching the paper 9 squares away. Draw a circle.

5. Put the point of your compass on the second dot and open it up until the pencil is touching the paper 5 squares away. Draw a circle.

6. Put the point of your compass on the third dot and open it up until the pencil is touching the paper 12 squares away. Draw a circle.

7. There should be only one point where all three circles meet. You've pinpointed a location!

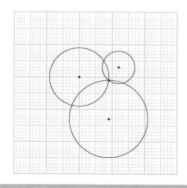

Puzzle activity

You're going on holiday! Can you find your way to the campsite? If your navigation device is broken, you'll need to find your own route. Follow the roads until you reach your destination. Just don't take a wrong turn!

START

FINISH

You'll find the answers at the back of the book.

Tap and swipe

You're at school now using a tablet computer. You can control one of these by touch alone: tapping, swiping, or pinching. But how does this actually work?

WOULD MY TOE WORK?

A tablet's display screen is covered by a touchscreen. Touchscreens take information (such as where your finger is on the screen) and send it to the device's processor (control center).

That's a similar job to a keyboard or mouse. But a touchscreen also has to be flat and see-through so it doesn't block your view of the screen.

protective cover

glass

transparent electrode film

Most tablets have a capacitive touchscreen. These are made of layers of thin glass and other materials. Electric currents flow through tiny wires that criss-cross inside the screen.

Your finger contains electric charges that affect the current when you touch the screen. An electronic circuit inside the tablet works out where this happened, and sends that information to the tablet's main processor. So that's how the tablet knows where your finger is!

A capacitive touchscreen works by changes in electricity rather than pressure, so it doesn't matter how hard you press on them. A light tap is enough!

gloves

HRMPH!

Gloves do not contain electric charges that can move around, so you can't operate a touchscreen if you are wearing them.

card

Giving a computer information or instructions is called inputting. Touching a screen is just one way to do this. You can also type on a keyboard, click with a mouse, or use voice commands. Long ago, people inputted by feeding computers cards with holes punched in them!

CLICK CLICK

mouse

TAP TAP

TAP TAP

keyboard

Make your own stylus

You will need:

- a ballpoint pen
- a cotton swab
- scissors
- sticky tape
- aluminum foil
- water
- a tablet or smartphone

A stylus lets you operate a touchscreen without touching it. Here's a quick way to make your own!

What to do:

1. Unscrew the ballpoint pen and remove the writing point and ink.

2. Cut a cotton swab in half.

3. Insert the cotton swab into the point of the pen. If it's hard to fit, try cutting it at an angle.

4. Tape the cotton swab in place. The tape shouldn't cover the soft part of the cotton swab.

5. Cut out a 2 x 2 in square of aluminum foil. Wrap it around the cotton swab and the neck of the pen. It must touch the soft tip of the cotton swab, but not cover it completely.

6. Secure the foil with tape.

7. Add a drop of water to the top of the cotton swab. The swab should be moist, not soaking.

8. Try your stylus on a phone or tablet. Make sure that your finger is touching the foil! If it stops working, add a bit more water.

Water contains electric charges that can move around freely, and so does aluminum foil. When you touch the foil, which is touching the wet cotton swab, electric charges move through the water and foil, and in your body. The moving charges mean that the touchscreen will work.

Puzzle activity

If you could design any app, what would it be? How would your apps make use of the device's touchscreen? Write a brief description for each of your three best ideas. Then design an icon for each.

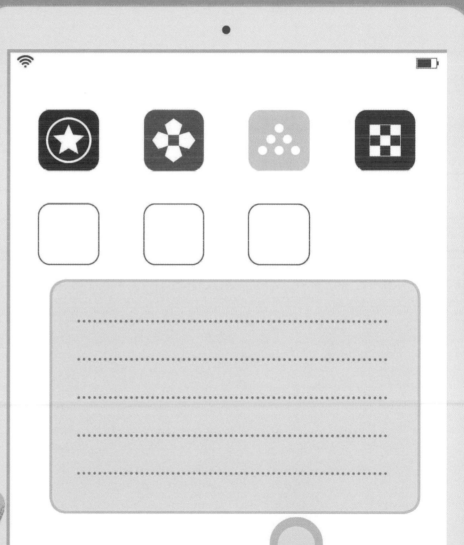

The write stuff

WHAT A MESS! START AGAIN!

When it comes to writing, it's hard to beat a pen. From ballpoints to felt-tips, pens let us get our ideas down on paper with a minimum of mess.

Long ago, people wrote with quills (feathers) or reeds (hollow stems) dipped in liquid ink. It was messy, because you had to keep dipping the pen in the ink, and the ink often got smeared before it could dry. In the 1800s, inventors perfected the fountain pen. It had a refillable ink container inside, so you didn't have to keep dipping.

In the 1930s, the inventor Laszlo Biro was tired of cleaning up smudges from his fountain pen. He knew that thick newspaper inks dried quickly, so he designed a pen that could use them. It had a tiny metal ball in the point that could roll around to spread ink. He'd invented the ballpoint pen.

metal ball

ink chamber

Felt-tip pens are useful for coloring, drawing and highlighting. They have a hollow plastic body and a writing tip made of soft fibers. Inside, a fiber cylinder holds the ink. The liquid ink travels down the fibers and to the tip. The ink includes alcohol, which helps it to dry quickly on the page.

Ink is a liquid or paste that contains pigments or dyes to give it color. Pigments are tiny solid colored particles. Dyes are colored substances that dissolve in a liquid. Pigments and dyes are what give paints and clothes color, as well as inks for pens.

colourful pigments

CHECK OUT THE DYES IN MY T-SHIRT!

Investigating ink colors

You will need:

- coffee filter paper (or paper towel)
- scissors
- "washable" felt-tip pens in different colors
- a glass tumbler or jam jar
- a pencil
- a paper clip
- water
- old newspapers

Sometimes colored ink is actually made up of several different colors. You can separate the colors out by using a process known as chromatography.

What to do:

1. Cover your work surface with old newspapers.

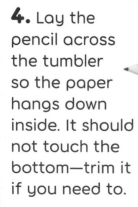

2. Cut the coffee filter into strips about 4 in long and 1 in wide. You will need one strip for each marker pen.

3. Loop the end of one strip around the pencil. Hold it in place with the paper clip.

4. Lay the pencil across the tumbler so the paper hangs down inside. It should not touch the bottom—trim it if you need to.

5. Take it out and draw a blob of ink about 1/2 in from the bottom. Put it back in the tumbler.

6. Carefully add water until it just touches the bottom of the paper.

7. Watch the water slowly rise up the paper. Take the strip out when the water is 1/2–1 in from the top.

8. Repeat steps 3–7 with the other pens.

You should see a mix of colors on the strips. The water has separated out the different substances in the ink.

Puzzle activity

Pens and markers come in all shapes and sizes. Each one in this picture has an identical partner—except one. Can you spot it?

Super scanners

On the way home from school do you ever stop at the store? At the checkout, you scan, pay, and go. But how does it work?

BEEP! BEEP!

Most shops have a database to keep a record of products sold. The database tracks every product's prices and stock levels. Each product has its own special number—and that's what a barcode is for. These black and white bars are a way of showing product numbers.

APPLE

NATURAL JUICE

0 36000

Each number is represented by 7 lines, either black or white. Sometimes two or more lines of the same color are next to each other to make a wider line. The code for "3" is 1 white line, 4 black lines, 1 white line, and 1 black line. The 4 black lines together look like one fat black line.

At the checkout, the scanner shines a laser onto the barcode. It reflects off the white parts of a barcode, but not off the black parts. A computer in the scanner recognizes the on-and-off pattern of light as the numbers in the barcode. It sends the numbers to another computer that holds the product database.

1. Laser beams onto barcode

2. Light reflects back off white parts of barcode

3. Scanner recognizes on-off pattern

4. Electric circuit turns on-off pattern into numbers

5. Computer recognizes number as a product code

10011

LASERS PRODUCE BEAMS OF CONCENTRATED LIGHT!

The shop's computer system keeps track of every product that is scanned at the checkouts. It works out which products are running low, so the store can order more.

Make your own barcode

You will need:

- graph paper with small squares (you will need about 70 squares for each row)
- a ruler
- a pencil
- a black pen
- a barcode key (see opposite page)

Barcodes are pretty simple things, once you know the code! Why not try making your own?

SCRIBBLE

What to do:

1. Choose a number between 5 and 10 digits long. It could be your birthdate, your phone number, or a random number.

2. Use your ruler and pencil to draw a straight line all the way across the graph paper.

3. Count down 10 squares and draw another line. Your barcode will be written between these two lines.

4. Find your first number on the key (below) and fill in the corresponding lines on your graph paper. Your "number" should be 7 squares wide. (Remember that two or more lines next to each other can look like a single, fat line.)

5. When you're sure you've got it right, color in the black lines with pen. They should each be 10 squares long, from top to bottom.

6. Repeat steps 4 and 5 for the rest of your numbers.

7. Write the numbers beneath the barcode lines, just like on a real barcode. Now you're ready to be scanned!

1 7 0 5 2 0 1 1

Puzzle activity

Decode this secret message! Use the key below to translate these barcode blocks into numbers. Then use the decoder to turn each number into a letter and read the message. (Hint: did you spot the white line at the start of each row?)

Decoder

0 = A
1 = C
2 = E
3 = I
4 = K
5 = N
6 = O
7 = R
8 = S
9 = !

Write your answer here:

....

....

Barcode key

| 0 | 1 | 2 | 3 | 4 | 5 | 6 | 7 | 8 | 9 |

A cellular world

Maybe you'll get home from school to find your mom talking to her office on her cellphone. We couldn't live without phones it seems, but how do these clever devices send and receive signals?

A cellphone sends and receives signals carried by radio waves. These are waves of electricity and magnetism that travel invisibly through the air at about 186,000 miles per second.

10:15

A cellphone doesn't just send radio signals directly to another phone. If lots of people in the same area tried to make calls at the same time, all those radio signals would interfere with each other!

city areas

rural areas

Instead, cellphones use a cellular network. Each cell in the network has a base station that sends and receives radio signals.

Cells in cities, where there are lots of people making calls, are smaller than cells in rural areas.

BEEP! BEEP!

40

2. Your phone transmits (sends out) a radio wave that has the digital signal encoded into it. The nearest base station picks up the radio waves.

3. The base station sends the digital signal (encoded as a radio wave) to the telephone network, which redirects it to the base station nearest your friend.

2

3

RING! RING!

1

4. Your friend's phone picks up the radio wave, recovers the digital signal, and changes that back into the sound of your voice!

4

1. Your phone converts your voice into electrical signals and then into strings of numbers (a digital signal).

DEET! DEET!

0208745

Landlines work in a different way. They have to be connected with wires, and electrical signals travel down those wires. You can't unplug a landline and take it out and about with you.

Blocking signals

You will need:

- a radio controlled car or other toy
- a pencil and paper
- materials to test: aluminum foil, plastic wrap, paper, fabric, rubber, yogurt cup
- lots of space

You cannot see or feel radio waves as they travel through the air—but you can block them! Try this experiment to find materials that block radio waves.

What to do:

check batteries!

1. Test the car and controller to make sure that the batteries are charged and it is working properly.

2. Take the first material you want to test and wrap it around the controller until it is completely covered. Use more than one layer.

completely cover aerial →

3. Try to drive the car with the controller. Does it work?

4. Make a note of your results.

5. Repeat steps 2–4 with the other materials.

2 3 4

Radio waves can travel easily through some substances, such as air. You probably found that radio waves traveled easily through some materials and the car still worked. Other materials, such as foil, block radio waves and reflect them back to the antenna.

Puzzle activity

Cellphones are everywhere today. In fact, there are more than 4 billion of them in use around the world! How many cellphones can you see in this picture? Count them and then colour the busy scene.

Snack time!

It's a while till dinner, so you pop a snack in the microwave. These metal boxes heat food quickly and safely, using some very clever technology. Ding!

PIZZA!

A standard electric oven has a heating element, similar to those used in toasters. The element heats up the whole box, cooking food slowly from the outside in.

A microwave oven is completely different. It sends waves of energy right into your food to heat it all the way through, cooking it quickly and evenly.

The world around us is full of waves of electricity and magnetism. We can see some of them as light, and feel others as heat. But there are many more waves that we can neither see nor feel. Microwaves are one of these. They are similar to radio waves, only more closely packed.

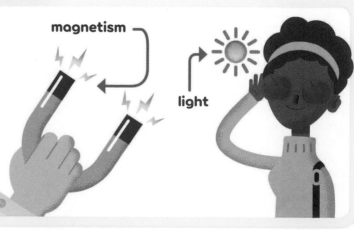

magnetism

light

Electromagnetic waves are categorized according to their wavelength (the distance from the top of one wave to the top of the next). The longest waves are radio waves. Next come microwaves. They are followed by infrared waves, which we can feel as heat. Then come visible light, ultraviolet, x-rays, and gamma rays, which are the shortest.

the electromagnetic spectrum

radio waves · microwaves · infrared · visible light · ultraviolet · x-rays · gamma rays

Food is made of very tiny particles called molecules. Molecules are always vibrating, and when microwaves hit them they vibrate more. A microwave uses electricity to produce microwaves. These blast into the food, making the molecules vibrate faster. This heats the food.

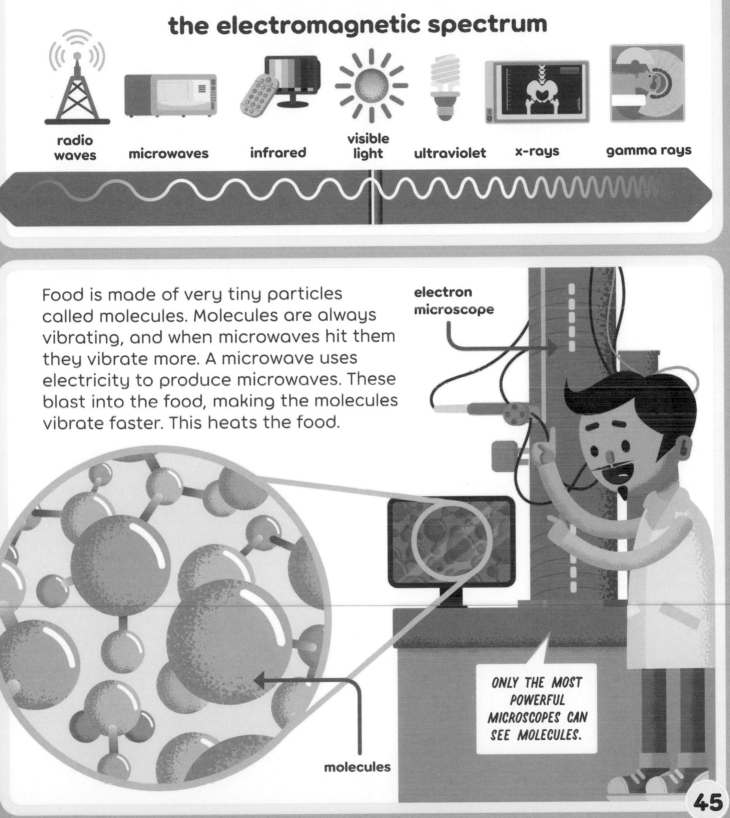

electron microscope

molecules

ONLY THE MOST POWERFUL MICROSCOPES CAN SEE MOLECULES.

Microwave heat test

You will need:
- an adult to help
- a microwave oven
- two flat-bottomed microwave-safe dishes
- marshmallows
- butter
- oven gloves
- a fork
- a pencil and paper

Does your microwave oven heat food evenly? Try this experiment to find out!

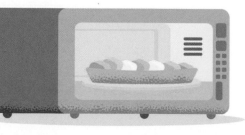

What to do:

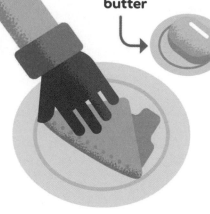

butter

1. Butter the sides and bottoms of both dishes, to stop the marshmallows sticking.

marshmallows

2. Fill both dishes with marshmallows, arranging them in tightly packed rows.

3. Put the first dish into the microwave and cook for one minute on low power. (If nothing happens to the marshmallows, try another 30 seconds.)

microwave

4. Ask an adult to take the dish out of the microwave. Poke the marshmallows with a fork and make a note of what you see. The marshmallows should be softer and stickier than before. Do they all feel the same?

5. Remove the rotating tray from the microwave and put the second dish in. Repeat steps 3 and 4 with the second dish.

The microwaves bounce around inside the oven, and in some places they combine, to give hot spots. Putting food on a rotating tray allows it to cook evenly. As your second dish didn't rotate, it should show where the hotter and colder spots are.

Puzzle activity

Different gadgets make use of different kinds of energy waves. Follow the lines to see which type of wave makes each gadget work.

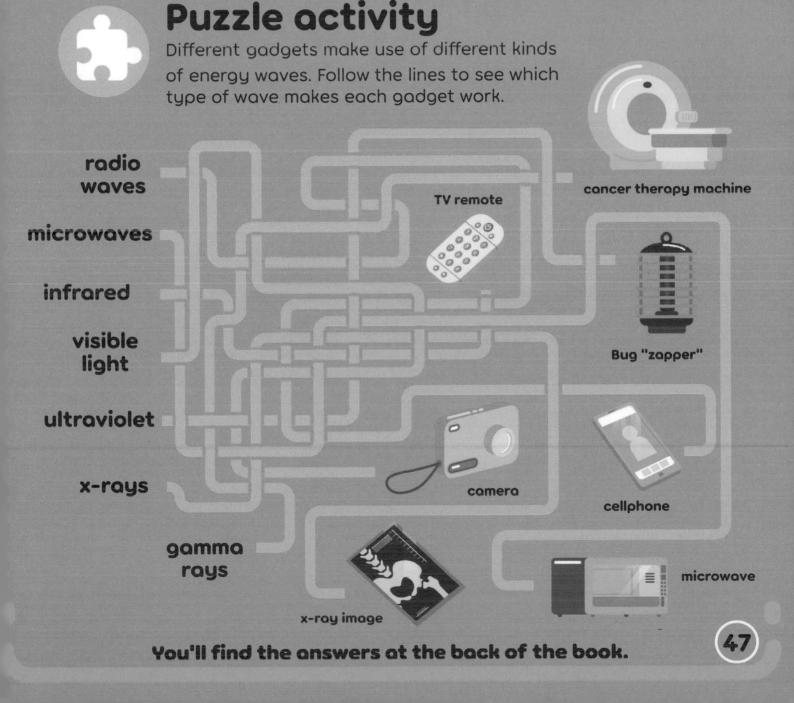

radio waves

microwaves

infrared

visible light

ultraviolet

x-rays

gamma rays

cancer therapy machine

TV remote

Bug "zapper"

camera

cellphone

x-ray image

microwave

You'll find the answers at the back of the book.

Helping out

Do you ever help your parents out by cleaning up a bit? Your job is most likely made easier by an electric vacuum cleaner, which sucks up dirt and mess no problem!

Vacuum cleaners rely on suction—the same force that lets you sip juice through a straw. They suck up dirt and dust, and trap it in a container, which you can later empty. Older vacuum cleaners use paper bags to trap the dirt. One kind of modern cleaner has no bag. It uses whirling air to separate dirt from clean air.

A vacuum cleaner uses a powerful electric motor to spin a fan that sucks in air, pulling it through the machine. Brushes and rollers loosen dirt from the floor so that it can be sucked in. Once the dust is separated out, the clean air flows out of the machine.

Inside the cone-shaped piece of plastic called the cyclone, dirty air swirls around at high speeds. The particles of dust are flung out to the sides. (This is similar to the way that washing machines spin fast to force water out of the clean clothes.) The dust drops to the bottom and collects in a plastic bin.

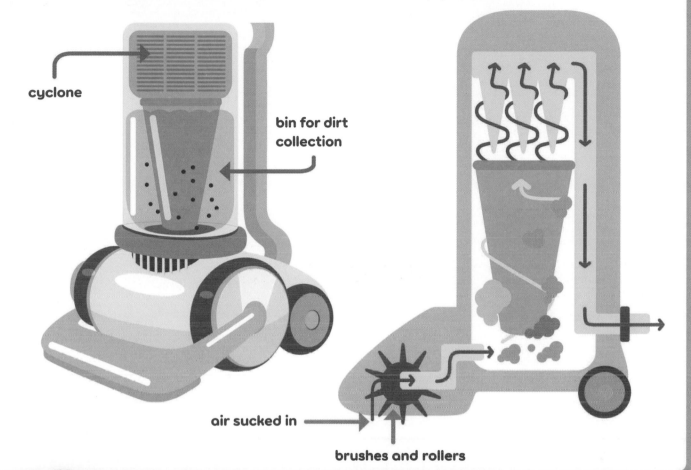

cyclone

bin for dirt collection

air sucked in

brushes and rollers

If a cyclone cleaner isn't high-tech enough for you, you can get a robotic one! These suck up dirt in the normal way, but they can drive themselves around the room, changing direction when they meet an obstacle.

Be a vacuum cleaner!

You can produce suction with your mouth and lungs—in fact, you do this every time you suck through a straw! You can use this amazing suction power to lift up dust and dirt.

What to do:

1. Wrap a piece of tissue paper around the comb.

2. Stand next to the armchair or cushion that you are going to try to vacuum.

3. Breathe out and try to get your lungs as empty as possible.

HUFF
PUFF

4. Quickly place the paper-covered comb against your mouth. Press the comb against the armchair or cushion, keeping your mouth touching the opposite side.

50

5. Suck in a strong breath, quickly and sharply. You should be breathing straight through the teeth of the comb.

SUCK!!!

6. Have a look at the tissue paper. Is it dirty?

When you breathe in, you suck up the air in front of your mouth. This creates an area of low air pressure. (Air pressure is how much the air pushes on a surface.) The air outside this area has higher pressure. It pushes in to fill the empty space. The tissue paper keeps the dust from going into your mouth.

Puzzle activity

Robotic cleaners run on battery power. After an hour or so of vacuuming, they need to be recharged. They do this by returning to the docking station, which plugs into an outlet. This robot cleaner must find its way back to its docking station. Can you find a path that will let it avoid obstacles?

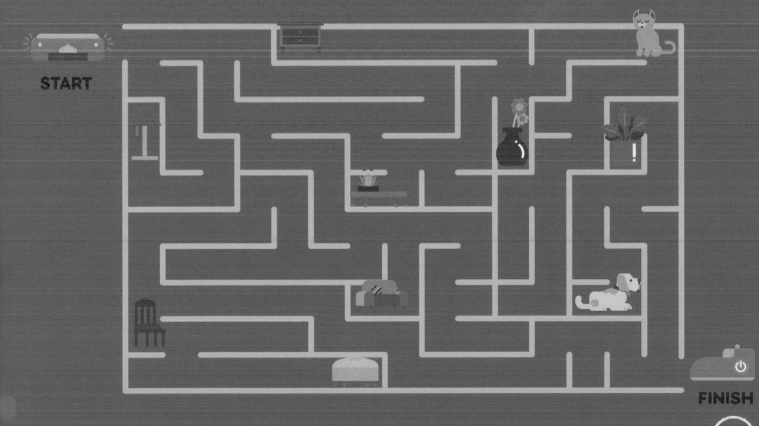

START

FINISH

You'll find the answers at the back of the book.

Simple machines

Before you go to bed there may be time for a quick bicycle ride. Bicycles make use of some very simple machines to get us from one place to another.

It takes a force (a push or a pull) to move or lift something. If it's something heavy, like a person, then it takes a lot of force. Simple machines help make these jobs easier. They can take a force and change its direction, make it stronger, or increase the distance it moves. A bicycle contains several different simple machines.

LEVERS

Handlebars are levers. If you push on one end of the handlebars, the other end moves in the opposite direction.

PULLEYS

The chain and gears act as a pulley system. Two pulleys are connected by a single chain. Turning one pulley, by pedalling, makes the other pulley turn. That second pulley turns the back wheel.

Ramps and wedges are also simple machines. You can pull something up a ramp instead of lifting it straight up. The gentler the slope of the ramp, the easier it is to pull (but the further you have to pull it!). Wedges help us push things apart.

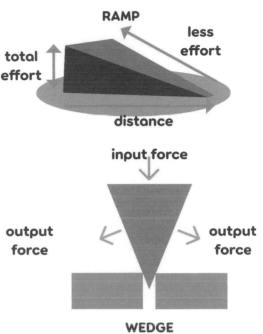

WHEEL

When two objects rub together, it creates friction. Friction is a force that slows things down. If the wheels didn't turn, the tires would simply rub against the ground, and the friction would prevent the bicycle from moving.

SCREWS

Screws help hold parts of the bicycle together. They take a force that goes around and around, and turn it into one that goes in and out.

Lifting with pulleys

You will need:

- an adult to help
- 3 carabiners (or strong curtain rings)
- a clothesline or rope
- a coat rack with hooks
- a bucket or empty paint can with household objects inside to act as weights

Pulleys don't just turn bicycle wheels. They can also help us lift heavy weights.

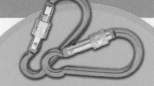

You can buy carabiners online or in an outdoors store. They are ideal for this project because they open and close.

What to do:

1. Tie one end of the rope to a carabiner, and clip the carabiner around the handle of your weight..

2. Feed the other end of the rope through one of the other carabiners, and hang the second carabiner from the coat hook. (Instead of a coat rack, you could use any other pair of solid fixed points.)

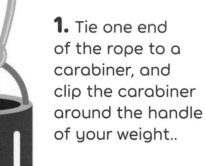

3. Pull down on the end of the rope. The bucket should lift up.

4. Unclip the carabiner from the bucket handle and hang it on one of the other hooks, next to the other carabiner.

5. Clip the third carabiner onto the rope, between the two other carabiners.

6. Pull the third carabiner down until you can clip it onto the bucket's handle.

7. Pull on the end of the rope again to lift the bucket.

Using two pulleys makes lifting easier. You have to pull the rope further to lift the bucket, but you do not have to pull as hard.

Puzzle activity

These scrambled words are the names of parts of a bicycle. Can you unscramble them and match them to the right part of the picture?

HEWLE

LEXA

ICHNA

EGRSA

NBHDASLREA

LDASPE

DASELD

You'll find the answers at the back of the book.

Bedtime brush!

SCRUBBB!

I PREFER THE NEW ONES!

Bedtime! Your last job before bed is to clean your teeth. We hardly notice them because we use them every day, but even toothbrushes are examples of brilliant technology!

Before the invention of toothbrushes, people chewed on sticks or used toothpicks to keep their teeth clean. The earliest device that looked like a modern toothbrush was invented in China. It had a bone or bamboo handle and bristles from a hog. Most modern toothbrushes are made with plastic handles and nylon bristles.

When you eat, bits of food get stuck on and in between your teeth. This can lead to a build-up of a sticky substance called plaque. Plaque contains microorganisms called bacteria that cause tooth decay and gum disease. Brushing your teeth removes plaque before it can cause harm.

Electric toothbrushes are thought to be better at removing plaque than manual ones. Inside the handle is an electric motor that spins quickly. The motor is connected to the brush head by a cam and gear unit. This unit turns the motor's spinning motion into a back-and-forth motion. It makes the brush head rotate back and forth to clean your teeth.

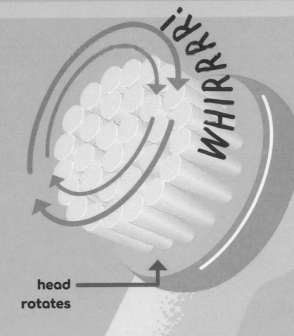

WHIRRR!

head rotates

cam and gears

The plastic case of an electric toothbrush protects the motor and battery from getting wet. The brush head comes off easily, so it can be replaced when the bristles wear out. The toothbrush stands on a plastic base when it isn't being used. The base plugs into the wall and charges the battery.

EVEN THE BEST TOOTHBRUSH NEEDS TOOTHPASTE!

motor

removable brush head

rechargeable battery

slides onto main unit

BZZZZZ!

Is electric better?

You will need:

- an adult to help
- 2 white eggs
- a saucepan and water
- a bowl
- fizzy brown soda
- a manual toothbrush
- an electric toothbrush
- toothpaste

Boiling water! WATCH OUT!

Companies that make electric toothbrushes claim that they do a better job of cleaning your teeth. With this experiment, you can put those claims to the test.

What to do:

1. Ask an adult to boil the eggs on the stove until the insides are solid. Let them cool.

2. Put the eggs in the bowl and pour in enough soda to cover them completely. Let them sit in the soda overnight.

3. Take the eggs out of the soda. Their shells should have turned brown.

manual toothbrush

4. Put some toothpaste on the manual toothbrush and use it to clean the brown stain off one of the eggs.

5. Repeat step 4 with the other egg, but this time use the electric toothbrush.

electric toothbrush

What results did you discover? Was the electric toothbrush better? Or were they both the same? Which toothbrush do you think is gentler on your teeth? Is that a good thing?

58

Puzzle activity

A dentist has sent you a secret message. Can you crack it? Each number or symbol in this secret message stands for a different letter. Use the decoder box to work out what it says.

Secret code

0 = A
1 = B
2 = C
3 = D
4 = E
5 = F
6 = G
7 = H
8 = I
9 = J
! = K
@ = L
£ = M
$ = N
% = O
& = P
* = Q
+ = R
/ = S
? = T
~ = U
< = V
> = W
÷ = X
∞ = Y
¶ = Z

Secret message:

1 + ~ / 7   ∞ % ~ +   ? 4 4 ? 7

? > 8 2 4   4 < 4 + ∞   3 0 ∞

The secret message says .....

....

....

Technology everywhere!

All day long, technology makes our lives easier. The experts who design our gadgets and machines continue to develop new technologies all the time.

Our earliest ancestors made stone tools. The wheel allowed people to move goods faster than before. The invention of the petrol engine changed things even more. Now jet-powered planes carry passengers around the globe.

New technology often starts with a simple idea about how to make a job easier. Teams of scientists, engineers, and designers work together to create a product. It often takes many years of patiently testing, tweaking the design, then testing again.

Think about what you've learned so far. Can you find other examples of technology in your daily life? Do you think you might design the world's next groundbreaking invention? Make sketches of your new idea. The sky's the limit!

Quiz time!

Test your memory to see if you can remember the answers to these questions about technology!

1. How do you tell the time on an analog clock?

a) reading the numbers on the display ☐

b) looking at the position of the hands ☐

c) counting the swings of the pendulum ☐

2. Electricity travels around a loop called a...

a) circuit ☐

b) conductor ☐

c) resistor ☐

3. How does yeast make dough rise?

a) it produces bacteria ☐

b) it gives off carbon dioxide that forms bubbles ☐

c) it changes sugars into acids ☐

4. What does GPS stand for?

a) Geography Program Satellites ☐

b) Government Protection System ☐

c) Global Positioning System ☐

5. Why did Laszlo Biro use newspaper ink in his new pen?

a) it was thick and dried quickly ☐

b) it came in lots of different colors ☐

c) it made it easier to refill the pen ☐

6. How many lines represent each number in a barcode?

a) 5 ☐

b) 7 ☐

c) 9 ☐

7. Cellphones send signals to each other in the form of...

a) sound waves ☐

b) x-rays ☐

c) radio waves ☐

8. What type of simple machine is a bicycle's chain and gear system?

a) pulley ☐

b) lever ☐

c) screw ☐

Answers: 1 b; 2 a; 3 b; 4 c; 5 a; 6 b; 7 c; 8 a

PUZZLE ACTIVITY ANSWERS

1. 12:34
2. 03:52
3. 07:13
4. 11:29

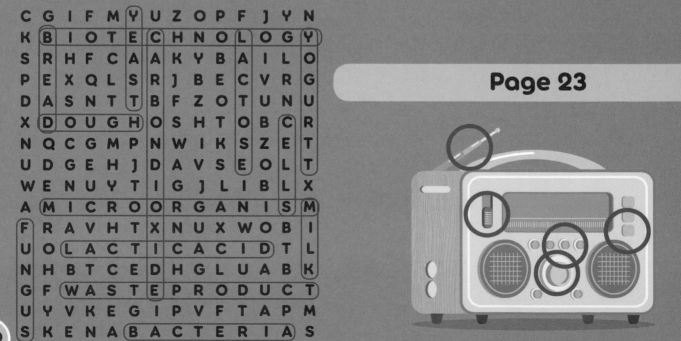

Page 19

C G I F M (Y) U Z O P F J Y N
K (B I O T E (C H N O L O G Y)
S R H F C A A K Y B A I L O
P E X Q L S R J B E C V U R G
D A S N T T B F Z O T U N U
X (D O U G H) O S H T O B (C R T
N Q C G M P N W I K S Z E E L T
U D G E H J D A V S E O L T
W E N U Y T I G J L I B L X
A (M I C R O O R G A N I S M) M
F R A V H T X N U X W O B I
U (O L A C T I C A C I D) T L
N H B T C E D H G L U A B K
G F (W A S T E P R O D U C T)
U Y V K E G I P V F T A P M
S K E N A B (A C T E R I A S)

Page 23

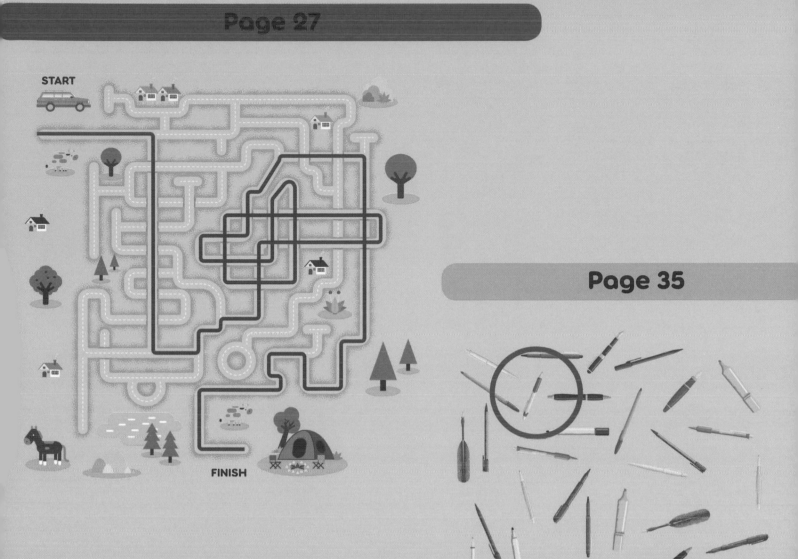

START

FINISH

8132512
761489
**SCIENCE
ROCKS!**

**There are 5 cellphones
in the picture.**

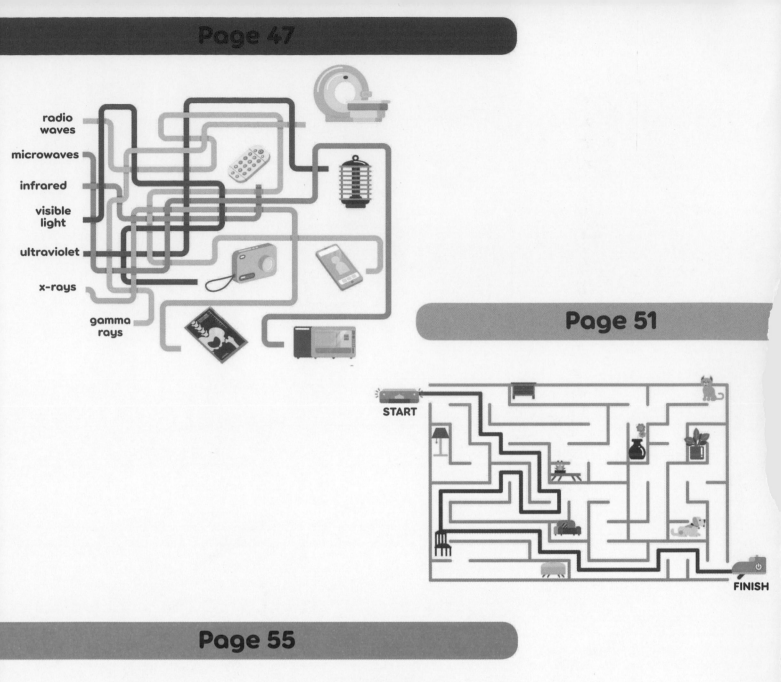

radio waves
microwaves
infrared
visible light
ultraviolet
x-rays
gamma rays

START
FINISH

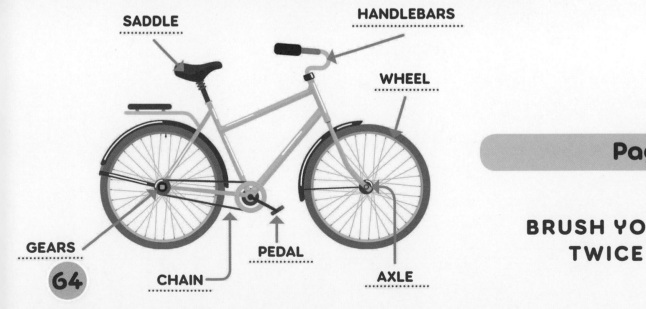

SADDLE
HANDLEBARS
WHEEL
GEARS
PEDAL
CHAIN
AXLE

BRUSH YOUR TEETH TWICE A DAY